D0439136

Calculator
Word
Games

NEW *EXPANDED* EDITION

Calculator
Word
Games

Bennie Rhodes

mott media
MILFORD, MI. 48042

The following items are used by permission. Copyright,
The Church Herald, 1977:
"The Anti-Christ?"
"The Tabernacle in the Wilderness"
"Golgotha"
"Consider the Flowers in the Field"
"The Devil and His Angels"
"They Received More than Knowledge"
"What an Awful Place!"
"John the Baptist"
"This Fellow Was Smart!"
"What Are These Strange Sounds?"

Robert Burkett, Editor

Library of Congress Cataloging in Publication Data
Rhodes, Bennie, 1927-
    Calculator Word Games (also entitled Bible Cal-
culator Word Games).
    SUMMARY: A collection of games related to the
Bible and biblical words played on electronic calculators.
    1. Calculating-machines—Problems,   exer-
cises, etc.—Juvenile literature. 2. Bible games
and   puzzles—Juvenile   literature. 3. Word
games—Juvenile literature. [1. Bible games and
puzzles. 2. Calculating machines—Problems,
exercises, etc. 3. Word games]
I. Title
QA75.R47   793.7   77-8870
ISBN 0-915134-39-X

This book is fondly dedicated to
  my children,
Dana and Leara,
who never had electronic calculators
when they were growing up;
but who had the Bible,
and learned to use it well.

Contents

Introduction:

How To Have Fun With Your Calculator and Your Bible

Welcome to the world of the electronic calculator! That marvelous little gadget you hold in your hand is designed to solve mathematical problems quickly and simply. You can use it in your school work, in the business world, in your everyday life to calculate all kinds of facts and figures.

But you can also have lots of fun with your calculator. This book presents simple mathematical puzzles which give an answer, not just in numbers, but in words too!

Have you already discovered your calculator can spell words? If you haven't, then let's do so now, so you can have fun with this book. Let me show you what I mean.

Take your calculator in hand and enter the number "3". Now, turn your calculator upside down and look at that number on the answer screen. Do you see how that number "3" looks like the letter "E" when it is viewed upside down?

Now enter the number "7" and look at it upside down. That looks like the letter "L", doesn't it? Put the number "8" into your machine next. That's the letter "B". The number "1" looks like the letter "I". Now add another "8" and, presto, you've spelled a complete word, "BIBLE".

Now you see how your calculator spells words! In this case the number 37,818, when viewed upside down, spells "BIBLE". Amazing, isn't it?

Many of the problems you will solve in this book are based on Bible words. Some will be names of characters found in the Bible, others will be words or ideas associated with the Bible. So you will want to keep your Bible handy as you work the problems to check how the words are used in the Bible.

Let me hasten to say, this is a fun book. The stories about Bible characters, words, and ideas are all fictitious. They are not

intended to express any Biblical truths.
There is no intention to cast an unfavor-
able light upon any character or incident
mentioned in the Bible. The problems are
designed simply to show how you can
have fun with numbers, especially if these
numbers lead you to uncover a name or
idea expressed in the Bible.

All the Scripture quotations, words, and
references in this book are taken from the
King James version of the Bible. If you use
any other translation you may find a different spelling of the Bible words, or discover that the word is not there at all because another word has been used in its
place. So use a King James translation in
checking your answers and references.

Each chapter begins with easy, warm-
up questions. The last few problems in
each chapter are the most difficult. Room
is provided in the margins for any calculating you may want to record.

The answers to all the problems are
printed at the back of the book. Don't peek
at the answers until you have worked the
problems. After all, there is no challenge

in a problem if you already know the answer.

Now you understand the purpose of this book, and how to use your calculator with your Bible, so you're ready to begin. Put some fresh batteries in that little magic box, and take off! May all your figuring have happy results!

Letter Equivalents:
1 = I
3 = E
4 = h (H)
5 = S
7 = L
8 = B
9 = G
0 = O

1

Searching for
Bible Characters

1. Walking In the Woods

Hannah was the mother of the great prophet, Samuel. When she went up to the House of the Lord to pray, she was embarrassed because she could not remember the name of the priest. So she thought, "Perhaps if I walk about in the yard, I will think of his name before I enter." With this in mind, Hannah took 27 steps toward the east. Then she turned north and counted 76 steps. Facing west she took another 54 steps, turned south and marched another 16. By this time Hannah was lost in the woods but at least she knew the name of the priest was _____
(1 Samuel 1:9).

2. An Ancestor for Joseph

Luke's account of the ancestors of Joseph, the husband of Mary, lists some strange sounding names. The one we are looking for is hidden somewhere in the pages of history and is only mentioned one time in the Bible.

Let's just assume he was a hard working man who labored in the vineyards. Suppose he earned 6 shekels a day on the job. He worked 270 days out of the year at that salary. But he also earned a share of the annual crop, which amounted to 133 shekels. How much did he earn that year? _____

When you find the answer you can read his name in the calculator. Look him up in Luke 3:25.

---

3. Caleb's Descendant

This man was a chief in the tribe of Judah, and he was descended from Caleb, one of the spies for Moses.

To find his name all you need do is divide the number of people in his tribe by 20. Let's say he had 5,804 families in his tribe and each family averaged 5 persons. Do you know the name of the chief? If not, look him up in 1 Chronicles 4:20.

---

4. Hosea's Other Name

I'll bet you didn't know Hosea had another name, did you? In the New Testament Paul used a different form for his name which you can find by working the following problem.

Hosea prophesied about 785 years before Christ. Paul wrote the book of Romans, in which his name for Hosea appears, about 60 A.D. If you will calculate all the seasons (Spring, Summer, Fall, Winter) in all those intervening years between Hosea and Paul, and subtract 30 from that total, you'll find Hosea's other name. _____ Look it up in Romans 9:25.

5. The Food Was Good!

When David was escaping from his son Absalom, he and his men were famished. He sent word to a man who was in charge of the city of Rabbah that he needed food desperately.

This man was anxious to please the king so he sent a group out with baskets to gather up food for the kings' troops. When they had finished gathering the food, the men carried the baskets to David and his starving soldiers. Someone counted the baskets and found there were 201 baskets and each basket had 90 pounds of food, except one which was only half full. When you calculate how many pounds of food they gathered you'll know the name of the man who supplied the food. If you have any trouble, look him up in 2 Samuel 17:27.

6. David's Mighty Men

King David had some of the bravest men in the world in his army. The one we're looking for is hidden somewhere in the list in 2 Samuel 23:8-39.

Suppose he was a spy with his name coded in numbers. To find his code number, enter the number 502,626 in your calculator. Divide that number by the number of days God used to create the world (Genesis 1:31) and subtract 37. See how easy it was to find his name? _____ Incidentally, he's listed in verse 29.

7. A Man Who Lived A Long Time Ago

A certain character mentioned in the Bible is said to have been born in the year 1130 B.C. If you add the number of years before Christ, and the number of years since Christ (1981), and multiply that by the days in a year, and subtract 397,801 from that number, you will discover his name was _____. He is mentioned in Judges 12:13.

8. A Fighting Man

This brave man was a captain in David's army. The Bible doesn't say much about him. In fact, his name is mentioned only once. But if he fought in David's army, you can believe he saw a lot of action.

We'll consider just three of the major battles he may have fought. First, there was the battle with the Philistines and in that battle Captain _____ commanded 27,900 valiant men. In another battle about a year later, this brave captain led 30,600 men. In his last major battle the captain could only muster 14,673 men, and because of this his army was forced to retreat. But if you add up all the men the captain commanded in the three major battles you will discover his name. Look him up in 1 Chronicles 11:46.

9. The Son of Zerubbabel

Zerubbabel led the first group of Israelites back to Jerusalem after their exile in Babylon. He had a son with an unusual name who helped him in his work.

Suppose Zerubbabel asked his son to be in charge of all the sheep herders who returned. They had a total of 190,840 sheep and each sheep herder could handle 26 sheep. How many sheep herders were there, and what was Zerubbabel's son's name? Check his name in 1 Chronicles 3:20.

10. David's Camel Driver

King David was a very wealthy man. Because he had lots of possessions, he needed men to oversee them. So he hired a man to take care of all his camels. You can find this man's name by discovering how many camels David owned.

Suppose this man went out to count the camels, but all he could see were the humps on their backs. He counted the humps with the plan of dividing the result by two, because he believed all camels had two humps. But someone wisely pointed out to him that some camels have only one hump.

"What can I do?" he cried. "I counted the humps, but now I don't know how many camels have two humps, and how many have only one hump!"

"The answer is very simple," replied the wise observer. "Lie down on the ground and count their legs. We know all camels have 4 legs."

Well, that's what the camel driver did. He counted 28,720 camels' legs. Figure the number of camels, and you'll know his name was _____.

Look him up in 1 Chronicles 27:30.

11. The King of Bashan's Bed

The ruler of Bashan was a powerful giant. He was defeated in battle by Moses and the Israelites in one of the great events in early Israelite history. What was so unusual about this king was his enormous bed. The Israelites talked about his bed for many years after his defeat.

Suppose his bed (called a sarcophagus) was 7.5 feet long, 6 feet wide, and 2 feet deep. Figure the cubic feet in that bed (ignore the zero after the decimal if it appears on your calculator) to discover the king's name. _____

Look him up in Numbers 21:33.

12. The Anti-Christ?

A preacher was trying to figure out the identity of the anti-christ, so he took the number 666 (Revelation 13:18), added the perfect number (12 × 12), and added the number of sheep that were not lost (Matthew 18:12). But he kept getting the name of a character mentioned in Revelation 20:8 instead!

---

13. Joseph's Father

Do you know the name of Joseph's father? I mean the Joseph who was the husband of Mary, the mother of Jesus.

Joseph was an honest man who always paid his debts. Now, the trick is, to find out what debts he paid.

First, he paid his taxes. This amounted to $60. Next, he paid his food bill, a total of $165. After this came a debt he owed for a donkey, $72. Then there was the rent for his carpenter's shop, $816. Then he decided he would pay his father $621 for teaching him to be honest. That's the payment that really paid off, because as soon as you put it into your calculator and touch the total button, you discover the name of Joseph's father. _____ He's mentioned in Luke 3:23.

14. Jehoshaphat's Grandfather

Jehoshaphat was one of the kings of Judah and he had a grandfather you wouldn't believe, unless you can imagine some things about him as I have.

The amazing thing about Jehoshaphat's grandfather was his ability to shear sheep. Why, that man could shear more sheep than a wool-gathering convention! Look at his statistics. He could shear 1,540 pounds of wool a day. Once, during a wool shearing contest, he sheared wool like that for 5 straight days and sold it for 19 shekels a pound. He also won 845 shekels as a prize for shearing the most wool.

If you find out how much money he earned, you'll see his name pop up in your calculator. Incidentally, he's mentioned in the Bible in 1 Kings 22:42 and 2 Chronicles 20:31. _____

15. This Name Will Amaze You

Way back in the early history of Israel there was a tribe called Asher. We're looking for the man who was the tribal leader, and who was also the son of Helem. Since we know very little about this man, we'll have to use our imagination to find his name.

Let's imagine he was a shepherd, as many people were in those days. He started out with 1,000 sheep. His flock doubled in size every year for 12 years. At the end of the 12 years he decided to sell his flock and retire. When he actually counted his sheep he had 441,345 more than he thought he had. How many sheep did he have, and what was his name? _____ You can look him up in 1 Chronicles 7:35.

16. Sons of Benjamin

Benjamin was one of the twelve sons of Jacob, and the Bible says he himself had ten sons. They were Belah, Becher, Ashbel, Gera, Naaman, Rosh, Muppim, Huppim, Ard, and _____. This problem gives the name of the tenth son.

The sons whose names begin with "A" had 11 children each. The sons with names beginning with "B" had 7 children each. Gera had 24 children, Naaman had 17, Rosh had 20, Muppim had 19, and Huppim, well, poor old Huppim had only 1. The son you're trying to find a name for had 26 children; if you add his family to those already counted, you'll know his name was _____. He is mentioned in Genesis 42:21.

17. The Builder of Jericho

In the days of Ahab, king of
Israel, lived a man who was fa-
mous for his buildings. It is said
that he rebuilt the city of Jericho.

Now this man was very
shrewd. He knew he could not
do the work alone, so he de-
vised a scheme to get the men of
Jericho to help him rebuild the
walls around the city. He promised that the young man who
earned the most points in the
building contest would be
eligible to marry his beautiful
daughter. He gave each man 6
points for every hour he worked
on the wall.

Simon really wanted to marry the builder's daughter. So he went to work. He worked straight through 18 hours a day, eating only one meal at night and sleeping about five hours. At the end of 67 days the wall was almost completed, so Simon decided to work right on through without stopping for 13 more hours.

He won the contest, married the builder's daughter, and of course lived happily ever after. Find his total points in the contest to discover the builder's name. _____ If you miss, look him up in 1 Kings 16:34.

18. How Lucky Can You Get?

One of the luckiest fellows in the Bible was King Ahasuerus' chamberlain. Listen to this story. The king decided that his queen, Vashti, could not reign any more because she had refused to parade her beauty before the people (see Esther 1:10–19). So he sent out a decree that all the young maidens in the land should come before the king so he could choose a new queen.

Now, it was the chamberlain's duty to interview all these beautiful young ladies and get them ready for their visit before the king. See how he lucked out!

Suppose the chamberlain had only 17 days to interview all of them. On the first day he interviewed 150 beautiful girls. But there were so many waiting to be interviewed that he decided to add 10 more the next day. He kept adding 10 more to the amount of the day before for 16 days. On the seventeenth day, he counted the number of ladies still waiting and found there were 334. So he interviewed all the rest that last day. If you can figure out how many young ladies this man interviewed in seventeen days, your calculator will give you his name.

_____ Otherwise, you'll just have to look him up in Esther 2:3.

19. Timothy's Godly Grandmother

You may already know the name of Timothy's grandmother. Paul mentioned her in one of his letters to Timothy and commended her for her faith. But if you would like to see her name pop up in your calculator, then consider the following:

Since Timothy's grandmother was a godly woman she prayed a lot during the years Timothy was growing up. Suppose she prayed 70 minutes each day during the first 12 years of Timothy's life (365.25 × 12). Figure the total number of minutes she prayed. Now convert the minutes to hours. Drop the numbers after the decimal by clearing your calculator at this point and putting just the whole number back into the machine. Subtract 6 from that number. Timothy's grandmother's name was _____. Verify your answer in 2 Timothy 1:5.

2

Searching for
Bible Words and Ideas

1. What An Awful Place!

If a man breaks all the estimated 7,733 commandments in the Bible and refuses to accept Jesus as Lord and Savior (that's one more), where will he likely go? _____

2. This Fellow Was Smart

In the parable of the unjust steward (Luke 16:1-8), Jesus told how the steward settled the accounts of his master's creditors. The steward found that five of the biggest creditors owed the following amounts: 138 shekels, 210 shekels, 307 shekels, 79 shekels, and 204 shekels. When he added up those amounts he was happy because he knew he would not have to do something he was ashamed to do. What was he ashamed to do? _____

3. Golgotha

If Jesus walked 5,354 miles in the regions of Galilee, traveled 964 miles by boat, and walked 1,396 miles in Gentile territories, where did it all end?

_____

4. The Tabernacle in the Wilderness

When Joshua and the Israelites were settling in the Promised Land, Joshua estimated that the Tabernacle had been moved 376,300 times while they were wandering in the wilderness, and another 30,845 times since they had crossed the Jordan River. So he decided to let the Tabernacle rest awhile at _
_____ (Joshua 18:1).

5. The Prodigal Son

Luke's Gospel tells the beautiful story of the prodigal son who went out into the world to live in sin, but finally realized how wrong he was and returned home to his loving father (Luke 15:11–24).

Let's suppose the prodigal son received the following amounts as an inheritance from his father: $1,260 in gold coins, $2,960 in silver, $1,500 in Jewish shekels, and $184 in Roman coins. The story tells us that the son went out and spent all that money and when he had spent all he had, he ended up feeding the _____!

6. John the Baptist

Though John the Baptist baptized great numbers of repentant people, he felt unworthy to baptize Jesus. Suppose John had baptized 3,045 persons in the Jordan River in the presence of a crowd of 50,000 onlookers. What garment symbolizes John's feeling of unworthiness? _____ Read the account in Mark 1:7.

7. The Serpent in the Garden

Genesis tells the story of the serpent who tempted Eve to eat the forbidden fruit (Genesis 3:1-6). Because of his part in the fall of man, the serpent was condemned to crawl on his belly and to eat the dust of the ground forever (Genesis 3:14 15). If you will work the following problem you will discover a word that has been associated with snakes ever since that day.

Suppose the Garden of Eden had 1,675 fruit bearing trees, 2,050 citrus trees, 1,275 shade trees, and 515 other assorted trees. Since Adam and Eve were told they could enjoy all the trees in the garden except 1, how many trees were there for them to enjoy, and what did the serpent say about that?

_____

8. Samson's Riddle

Samson asked a riddle about a beast of the field, an insect, and the product of an insect. His riddle went like this: "Out of the eater came forth meat, and out of the strong came forth sweetness" (Judges 14:14). Now let's suppose that the meat in Samson's riddle, if purchased at today's supermarket prices, would cost $46.98, and suppose the sweetness would cost $6.40. If you add that up you will discover the third part of Samson's riddle—the name of the insect—and you can look up the answer to the rest of the riddle in Judges 14:8–14. _____

9. Everyone Should Read This Book

The book that Jimmy was reading had 66 different sections, and he figured it would take an average of 5.73 hours to read each section. What book was Jimmy reading? _____

10. The Devil and His Angels

The devil and his angels were cast out of heaven (Revelation 12:7–9). Suppose he had 12 legions of angels, each legion numbering 5,862 angels. Where did they go? (Don't forget to count the devil.) _____

11. The False God

The Babylonians had many false gods, or idols. One of their chief gods was housed in 41 temples scattered through the country and each temple had 18 marble steps. Calculate the number of marble steps in all the temples to discover the name of the idol. Then look him up in Isaiah 46:1. _____

12. What a Place for a Battle!

It seems David and the Philistines were always battling it out
somewhere. One of their battles
took place after the men had
marched all day and pitched
their tents for the night. David
had 3,232 men with him and
they decided that 4 men could
sleep in each tent. Of course,
there was 1 extra tent for David.
How many tents did they pitch?
The answer will give you the
name of the place where they
fought the battle. It's mentioned
in 2 Samuel 21:18. _____

13. Moses' Ultimatum

When the children of Israel were slaves in Egypt, God sent Moses to Pharaoh to ask him to let the people go. On several occasions Moses issued ultimatums to Pharaoh, threatening to send plagues upon him if he refused to let them go.

One of those ultimatums went like this: "Let my people go, that they may serve me. _____, if thou refuse to let my people go, behold, tomorrow will I bring the locusts into thy coast" (Exodus 10:3–4).

Locusts were a kind of grasshopper that could literally eat up everything in sight. Suppose the millions of locusts that came into Egypt could devour 148.875 acres of vegetation in one hour. How many acres of land would they devour in one 24 hour day? When you find the answer, fill in the blank with the word you see.

14. Ahithophel's Hometown

Ahithophel was David's chief counselor. When David's son, Absalom, rebelled against his father, David sent for Ahithophel. The Bible doesn't tell us what advice Ahithophel gave David, but it does give us the name of his hometown, and that's what we're looking for.

Let's suppose Ahithophel told David he needed to muster an army of 13,500 men to put down the rebellion. Each man would be armed with a sword and a bow, and supplied with 3 arrows. In addition to this, a special chariot would carry 219 extra arrows, one for each officer in the army. If you will figure up how many arrows they had to shoot, you'll get an extra bonus and discover the name of Ahithophel's hometown. Look it up in 2 Samuel 15:12. _____

15. More Than Knowledge

The Rev. James Smith challenged his congregation to read the Bible through in one year by telling them that the Bible contained a sum of 31,101 verses. A total of 172 people enlisted in the Bible-reading program, including Mr. Smith. At the end of the year all the people had finished reading all the verses, and Mr. Smith had read 6,006 extra verses for good measure. When he added up all the verses, he discovered what God does for us every time we read the Bible. _____

16. The Walls of Jericho Came Tumbling Down

If you read the account of the fall of Jericho in Joshua 6:1–20 and use your calculator with a little imagination, you will know what action Joshua and his people took against the city.

Suppose Joshua had a total of 151,213 people in his army, including himself. Now all these people marched around the city once each day for 6 days, and 7 times on the seventh day. Calculate how many trampling feet went around the city on all those trips to find that mysterious word which describes what they were doing to the city. _____

Or figure it another way. Suppose every man in Joshua's army shouted at the proper time (verse 20) and each man's shout had a wind velocity of 26 miles per hour. Calculating the force will give you the word you're searching for. _____

17. The Cry From the Cross

While Jesus was hanging on the cross, dying for our sins, He said some very significant things. One of His sayings was a quotation from Psalm 22:1, "My God, my God, why hast thou forsaken me?" But Jesus spoke in Aramaic. What word is "My God" in Aramaic?

Put the number of words in Psalm 22 in your calculator (521). Subtract the number of words actually quoted by Jesus. Multiply that number by 2 and add the perfect number (7 × 7) to your answer. Your magic calculator will tell you that the Aramaic word for "My God" is _____. Check it out in Mark 15:34.

18. Goliath

The Philistine giant Goliath challenged the armies of Israel (see 1 Samuel 17:1–10). He was 10.5 feet tall. His armor weighed 150 pounds, his spearhead weighed 20 pounds. Goliath himself weighed about 622 pounds. If you convert his height to inches and add that in with all the weights, you will see that Goliath was indeed a _____ man!

19. Job's Afflictions

Job was a great man in the Old Testament. When the Lord gave Satan permission to test Job's faith, Job lost everything he owned and his body was covered with ugly sores. Three friends, Eliphas, Bildad, and Zophar, came from great distances to comfort him. Their immediate concern was to find out what those sores were on Job's body.

Eliphas thought he could find the answer in the stars. So he counted all the stars he could see, which was 2,079, and multiplied that number 7 times.

Then Bildad put forth his theory. He thought the answer lay in how many miles they had all traveled to get there. He found out that Eliphas had traveled 331 miles, he himself had traveled 296 miles, and Zophar had traveled 452 miles. He multiplied this total by 10 because he believed 10 was a magic number. But he too failed to get an answer.

Zophar believed the answer could be found by questioning the inhabitants of the town where Job lived. So he made up a list of 5 questions, and asked 6,353 residents for their opinion on each question. But when he tallied all this up, he was still perplexed by Job's illness.

Finally, another friend came along, a wise young man. When the three friends told him of their frustration, he said to them, "My friends, you simply didn't go far enough in your calculations. If you add together all three answers you received, you'll find that Job's body is covered with _____!" (Job 2:7).

20. Which Way Is Up?

Where is God's dwelling place located?

Multiply the number of feet in a mile by the number of inches in a foot; divide by the number of feet in a yard, and subtract 16,206. That should tell you where God dwells, and if you have any trouble you can look it up in Psalm 113:5. _____

21. This One Is Taxing

In the days when Jesus was born, during the reign of Caesar Augustus there went out a decree that all the people should be taxed (see Luke 2:1–3). When the taxing of all the territories was over, King Herod's tax collector reported to the king the following sums; Judea, 12,575,200 shekels; Samaria, 15,490,515 shekels; Galilee, 31,026,743 shekels. If we suppose that a shekel was equivalent to $00.64 (64¢) in our money, you can understand why the king said, "If this keeps up, all our people will be _____ for the poor house."

22. Stretching the Truth

All people should always tell the truth. But if you would like to discover an Old Testament word that means "to lie", then consider the following:

Just for fun, a group of boys and girls at a camp retreat were telling tall stories before bedtime. Roger told about the summer he worked as a lumberjack. He said that with his magic chainsaw he could cut down 345 trees a day! Now, Roger only worked as a lumberjack during the months of June, July, and August. On the last day of August he only cut 343 trees because he ran out of gas for his chainsaw. If you figure up how many trees Roger cut (assuming he worked every day during those three months) you'll find the word we're looking for. _____ If you want to see how it's used in the Bible, look it up in Jeremiah 5:12.

23. Consider the Flowers of the Field

Ed, the florist, was doing his sales records for 1976. He had worked every day, except Sundays, throughout the year. He found that his sales of a certain flower had averaged $16.48 for every day he had worked, and when he added the $142.45 he had collected for sales tax, his magic calculator told him the name of the flower. Don't forget 1976 was a leap year. If you have any trouble with this one you can look the answer up in Matthew 6:28. _____

3

Having Fun
At the Church

1. A Sad Story

The men of the church were engaged in constructing a youth building in the backyard of the church grounds, using concrete blocks.

They started with one wall which required 161 blocks laid end-to-end for each layer. When they had completed 5 layers, the pastor came by to check on their progress.

"I hate to tell you this," he said, "but the wall is not straight. You'll have to tear it down and start over."

The only sound from the hard-working men was one big

_____ _____.

2. Land Hungry

At a recent church party someone asked the identity of a newcomer to the group. "Oh, that's Farmer Benson," the pastor replied. "He just bought 2,000 acres of land down the road."

"Yeah," spoke up one of the ladies standing by. "And I heard he bought 340 acres from my neighbor."

"That's nothing," added Farmer Brown. "He bought 2,175 acres from my cousin."

"That isn't all," said another. "He bought 794 acres from Farmer Jones just last week."

"Well," said the person who had asked the question in the first place. "It sure seems like this fellow _____ around gobbling up all the land he can get!"

3. A Disaster!

Janet wrecked her car on the way to the church picnic. A kind garage man towed her car in for repairs and a friend picked her up and drove her to the picnic. When Janet went back to the garage to get her car, she asked, "How much is it?"

"Well," the garage man replied, "for fixing the headlight, $10.31, for repairing the bumper, $25.80, and for repairing and painting the fender, $26.07. And there will be a tow charge of $15.00 added to all that."

When Janet added all that up, she almost fainted at the size of the _____.

4. Church Musician

Jack was getting ready to perform in the annual church Christmas music program, so he practiced on his musical instrument 1 hour and 10 minutes every day for 44 days. How many minutes did Jack practice and what instrument did he play? _____

5. Special Entertainment

A certain man used to travel around the country visiting different churches with special entertainment. During one week this man appeared in 5 different churches and the average offering collected for him in each church was $101.41. If you've been working your calculator, you already know this man was singing _____!

6. That's a Lotta' Books

A certain young lady in the church was an avid book reader. In one summer vacation period she kept a list of all the books she had read with the number of pages in each book. At the end of the summer she found she had read 39,851 pages in 98 books! If she continues to do this every summer during her high school years and every summer during her college years, how many pages would she read? _____ When you find the answer to this one, you will also discover the girl's name! _____.

7. This Preacher Got Around!

An old-fashioned preacher who lived many years ago was known for his traveling. He preached at revival meetings in almost every state in the nation. In the last 25 years of his life he traveled an average of 19,655 miles a year going to his revivals.

The remarkable thing about it is that the preacher didn't have an automobile. He traveled all those miles in an old-fashioned, one horse _____!

8. Who's Keeping the Books?

A certain young lady was the treasurer of her church. She found that the average offering for each Sunday in the year was $6,077. When she tallied up the total offerings for the year and added the $1,714 special offering for missions, she discovered the calculator had revealed her name. What was it?

---

9. The Handshaker

Sam: What would you say about a preacher who shakes hands with an average of 4,882 people twice each Sunday of the year?

Bo: Add 6 more to the annual total and I'll say that's an awful lot of _____!"

10. The Church Parsonage

In England a special word describes the land where the church parsonage is located.

Suppose the church purchased 3 acres of land at $4,100 per acre and built a parsonage on the land which cost $26,079. Find their total investment and you'll discover the word you're looking for. _____

11. What A Church Can Do

David's church had a total budget last year of $13,832. If you will divide that number by the number of weeks in a year, and divide that number by the number of days in a week, you will discover that a church can _____ whatever it wants.

12. What Are Those Strange Sounds?

Joe Brown attended church once each Sunday for 10 consecutive years. On his way to church he kept feeling and hearing strange vibrations in the air. After he had counted them for several Sundays, he found that he felt and heard an average of 111 vibrations each Sunday. Allowing for a miscount of an additional 18 vibrations, he discovered he had been hearing

_____

13. The Lost Sermon

The preacher was working in his study on Saturday night, typing his sermon for the next day. He had worked hard on it and thought it was one of the best he had ever written. The only problem was that it was a bit too long. He counted the pages. There were 25 full pages with 300 words on each page. The last page, page 26, was not a full page, so the preacher counted the exact words on that page and found there were 215.

Still, it was a good sermon so he closed the window in his study and went home to bed.

The next morning, the preacher could not find his sermon, though he searched everywhere. Of course, if you've been working with your calculator correctly, you already know he left it on the window _____ the night before!

14. The Right Word

A pastor was trying to illustrate a sermon about the farmer in the New Testament who kept building bigger barns until one day the Lord told him he was a fool because he would die that very night (Luke 12:16–20). The pastor wanted to use a modern illustration and kept referring to those tall, cylinder-like buildings farmers use to store corn. But he couldn't think of their name. He described them this way:

"If you took all the corn that is raised in our county, which is about 304,290 bushels, you could store 1/6 of it in a pair of those structures."

One of his members, sitting on the front row, took out his pocket calculator and after a little fast figuring, he yelled out, "Preacher, the word you're looking for is _____!"

15. Mysterious Occupation

The pastor's wife was forced to seek employment to help make ends meet. When asked what kind of work his wife is doing, here's what the pastor says:

"Well, first, you have to understand something about her background. You see, my wife came from a family which settled in Kentucky many years ago. At first, the family bought 80 acres of land. Then later, they acquired another 50 acres, and, finally, they bought 215 more acres which gave them a total of _____ acres.

"Then you have to understand that it takes a lot of clothes for a pastor's wife. Last year, for instance, my wife spent $346.25 for dresses, $162.10 for coats, $25.72 for hats, and $43.28 for shoes. That means her clothing bill was $ _____

"Finally, you have to understand that a pastor's wife needs to feel that she is contributing something. Since she is working only part-time, her pay will not be a large amount, but it will help. For instance, she wants to earn enough to pay for our vacation. That will amount to 20% of her total pay of $2,652.25, or $ _____."

Since the pastor never did get around to telling us what his wife does, you'll just have to figure it out for yourself on your little calculator! _____

16. Plastered With Money!

Every artist worth his salt has worked with plaster of Paris, a chalk-like substance used to prepare a surface for painting, or to make a sculpture. But there's another word for that substance which you can find in your calculator in a plural form if you find the right answer to this problem.

Suppose an artist wanted to paint a mural for the church. To pay him for his beautiful work, the church asked each one of its 2,750 members to contribute $1.75. In addition, the church gave the artist an extra $242.89 to pay for his materials. If you figure out how much money the artist received, you'll find the word for plaster of Paris.

17. What's He Doing?

Suppose you are arriving at the annual church picnic held on Saturday, July 22, and you notice this strange man standing by the long table waving his arms frantically. You wonder what he's doing, so you take out your pocket calculator and do some figuring on the spot.

The man is 61 inches tall, weighs 189 pounds, and is 51 years old. You add all these figures together and multiply by the day of the month. Then you multiply that figure by the day of the week. Then you add 3,691 to this total—the estimated number of hours the ladies spent preparing all that delicious food. What does all that have to do with the man waving his arms? Why it's simple. This man _____ flies!

18. That Should Make It Shine!

The men of the church decided the church needed painting. So they formed a committee to get the job done. The committee came back with a report on the cost of the project. They figured it would take 60 gallons of paint at $7.95 per gallon, 21 paint brushes at $3.00 each, and assorted other items such as scrapers and thinner which amounted to $10.79. But they were enthusiastic about the results of a new paint job. They said, "Men, it will be worth it just to see our church shine with a new _____!"

19. Happily Married

Grandpa and Grandma Jones celebrated their 65th wedding anniversary at the church. While Grandma was talking to all the visitors, Grandpa was playing with the new calculator his children had given him. He added up the ages of all their 13 children and found that their average age was 54.5 years. Then he calculated the average age for their 37 grandchildren to be 30.2 years. Next, he added up the ages of their 62 great-grandchildren and found the average to be 11.4 years. Then Grandpa guessed that the average age of the 49 friends who had called was 57.5 years. Finally, Grandpa entered his age as 84.8 years, and Grandma's age was 82.8 years.

When Grandpa Jones added all these ages together, he found that he and Grandma had enjoyed 65 years of wedded

4

Having Fun
With People

1. Cover Him Up!

Helen's baby brother was old enough to sit in his high chair and eat his cereal. But he kept ruining his clothes by spilling all that mush on them. First, he ruined a shirt which cost $3.98. Then it was a pair of pajamas which cost $2.79. Again he ruined another shirt which cost $1.41. Helen added up the cost of all those garments and suggested to her mother that baby brother ought to wear a

_____

2. He Couldn't Work That Day

In a certain company there were 10 senior executives, 20 junior executives, 21 secretaries, and 721 other employees. On January 3, 1977 they all showed up for work except 1. That was the janitor, who called in and said he was

_____

3. She's a Mean Woman

Judy had refused to date 335 men, slapped the faces of 475 other men, and kicked the shins of 7 more. She defended her actions by saying it was all a part of women's _____.

4. Achilles Had a Tender Spot

Achilles was his name. He ran 3,762 miles through the desert, 2,531 miles in the valleys, and another 1,041 miles over the mountains before he was finally brought down by a shot in the

_____.

5. He Traveled a Lot

Monte was figuring his expenses for a recent trip. He had spent $21,560 for tickets, $11,404 for meals, $604 for tips, and $4,511 for extras. That all added up to a very large amount. But Monte did not complain. After all, he had been around the _____.

6. How's That Again?

A big, heavy farmer stopped at a restaurant for breakfast. The waitress came up to his table to take his order.

"May I take your order, please?" she asked.

"I'll have 2 dozen scrambled eggs, 15 biscuits, and 4 slices of country ham," replied the hungry farmer.

When the waitress received such a tall order, she gulped, "_____?"

7. What A Job!

Bill was offered a job which would pay him a total of $54,108 per year. When he divided that figure to see what he would earn each month, all he could say was, "_____!"

8. Too Many Chiefs

Two Indians went to Washington D.C. to straighten out some tribal affairs. On a day off they toured the city. Visiting the Capitol, they asked how many people worked there. A guard told them, "Well, we have 493 congressmen, 100 senators, and 11,576 staff people working for them."

At the Pentagon they asked the same question. "We have 57,102 people working in this department," they were told.

Another department employed 276,593 people. The Treasury Department had 176,936 people. Their final stop was the White House where they learned that 12,708 people worked for the President.

When the tour was over, one of the Indians turned to the other and remarked, "No wonder our country is in trouble. We've got too many _____!"

9. Facts Don't Mean A Thing

Two students were discussing the merits of solar energy. Bobby was carefully explaining how it could save energy in the average house.

"Look," he said, "suppose you were using 3,750 kilowatt hours of energy a month, and suppose you installed a solar energy system and it provided for you 2,842 kilowatt hours of energy per month. The difference between those two figures would be the amount you would have to pay for energy, which amounts to only 24.2% of the total energy used!"

To this, Eugene replied, "Please don't _____ me down with so many facts. Just give me the figures and let me decide for myself."

10. Traveling Men

Sandy answered the door bell to find two strange men, with tattered clothing and whiskers, standing at her door.

"Could you please let us have something to eat?" they pleaded.

"Who are you?" asked Sandy.

"We're traveling men, Miss. You see, we have traveled all over the world. Why, just last year we traveled 27,000 miles by train, 15,000 miles by car, 5,304 miles by boat, and 3,500 miles walking."

"You must be awfully tired after all that traveling," said Sandy. "Come on in."

After feeding the men, Sandy got her calculator and added up all those figures, and discovered the men were

_____!

11. Silly Girl

Bobby was angry at his girl friend, Edna. While courting her he had spent $1,574.50 for flowers, $269.00 for perfume, $1,500.00 for clothes, $455.69 for telephone bills, and now, while he was proposing marriage, all she could do was _____.

12. A Staggering Thought

When Jim read in the newspaper that 21 millionaires had paid only $79,780.68 in federal taxes, for an average payment of only _____, all he could say was, "Man, that sure does _____ my mind!"

13. New Boy in Town

A new family moved in next door to Richard, and since they had a son his age, Richard went over to get acquainted.

"Hello," he said to the new little boy. "What's your name?"

"Karl," replied the new kid. "We came from Germany."

"Oh," replied Richard, "would you teach me some German?"

"Yes," answered Karl. "Where do you want to start?"

"How do you say, 'Hello'?" asked Richard.

"Well," said Karl, "we have several ways to greet people. One of them is similar to your greeting. Suppose you take the calculator number for "hellos" which is 507,734, subtract 15,488, and divide that number by 69. Turn your calculator upside down and you will see our greeting."_____

14. A Beautiful Girl

Here's a poem Johnny wrote
for his girl friend on Valentine's
Day:

> If I sent you a hundred
>   kisses,
> Every day this year,
> Would not be enough to
>   show my love,
> To you, my lovely dear.
>
> So, on this Valentine Day,
> I'm sure you can tell,
> I've included 1,238 more
>   kisses,
> To describe my lovely
>
> _____!

15. Make a Joyful Noise

Tommy picked up a song book one day and began looking through it. He found there were 61 songs in the book and the average number of notes in each song was 55. He also discovered a little chorus in the back of the book that had 24 notes in it. When Tommy figured up all those notes he decided it was time for him to join the club.

16. This Man Is Hungry

Sam: How would you describe a man whose daily caloric intake of food is 12,300 calories a day for 364 days in the year, and 42,704 calories on Thanksgiving Day?

Bo: I would have to say he is _____!

17. These Ladies Have a Problem

At a recent meeting of over-weight ladies, 15 ladies weighed in at 135 pounds, 12 at 141 pounds, 35 at 150 pounds, 32 at 155 pounds, 43 at 160 pounds, 31 at 165 pounds, 27 at 170 pounds, 15 at 175 pounds, 6 at 180 pounds, 3 at 185 pounds, 2 at 190 pounds, and 1 at a whopping 228 pounds! How would you describe these ladies? _____

18. Televisionitus!

Sam: What would you say to a kid who started on Monday and watched television 360 minutes every school day during the week for 3 weeks, and 652 minutes on each Saturday and each Sunday for the 2 weekends?

Bo: I'd say to him, "You're a _____ for watching the tube that much!"

19. What A Job He Has!

At the beginning of 1977 Farmer Brown found the first business invoice he had written, dated Jan. 1, 1943. He had been in business _____ years.

Then he decided to figure the miles he had traveled taking his product to market. He averaged 8 trips a month for the years he had been in business, and each trip was exactly 17.5 miles. He had also taken his product to a sales convention in a distant city and the total mileage for that trip was 615 miles. How many miles had he traveled taking his product to market? _____

Next, Farmer Brown computed his average profit per year. His total profits for all the years he had been in business was $203,762. It was easy for him to find his average profit per year:

_____

Solve all three problems to discover what Farmer Brown does for a living! _____

96

5

**Having Fun
With Animals,
Gadgets and Things**

1. He Didn't Catch Much

David spent $4.52 for bait, $1.79 for new lures, and $1.02 for corks. He was disappointed though, because all he could catch that day was an _____.

2. Call Him Something

Sam: How would you describe an animal that eats 126,600 pounds of food one day, 126,700 pounds the second day, and 126,609 pounds the third day; and then sits around for six months staring at the world?

Bo: I would call him a _____ eyed monster!

3. He Was a Smooth Talker

David was telling Sue and Tommy a bedtime story. The story went like this:

Once upon a time there were three bears who lived in the forest. One day, when things were pretty dull, Baby Bear said to Mommy Bear, "Let's have a party and invite lots of people, uh, I mean animals."

Mommy Bear asked Papa Bear if it would be all right for them to have a party and invite a few guests. Papa Bear said it would be fine as long as they brought their own refreshments. So, Baby Bear went out into the woods and began inviting friends. She invited 376 elephants, 1,562 monkeys, 79 hippopotamuses, 1,750 squirrels, 2,089 rabbits, 1,915 birds, and 408 turtles.

Now, after hearing a story like that, how would you describe the manner of David's speech?

_____

4. How's This for Dessert?

Mary was helping her mother cook supper. She watched her mother as she put ingredients into the electric mixer. She noticed that the mixer was set on a slow speed of 369.5 revolutions per minute. Her mother timed the mixing of the ingredients to exactly 2 minutes. Then she set the bowl in the refrigerator and said to Mary, "Now, we will just wait and let it _____."

5. The Mysterious Holes

If a man had been digging 10 holes in the ground, each one 71 feet deep, what was he looking for? _____

6. Wild Crowd

At a recent ballgame there were 36,962 people in attendance. When the quarterback scored a touchdown 31,954 fans stood to their feet cheering. What sounds were coming from the rest of the fans? _____

7. What a Gander!

This bird is not mentioned in the Bible, but if you plucked enough of his feathers to stuff 1,000 mattresses with 35 pounds of feathers in each mattress, and had 9 pounds left over, you would know he was a mighty big _____!

8. The Fields Are White

Janet's uncle was growing some strange looking plants in the fields. She noticed that each plant had an average of 4 blooms. Suppose there were 274 rows in the field with an average of 49 plants per row. Add 4 extra blossoms to the total. Janet was counting cotton
_____.

9. Cry Baby

"What does the baby doll say when you pull the string?" asked the nursery worker.

"It says, '1,059 + 3,759 × 658 + 1,833,764' " was Amy's reply.

What's that? _____

10. Strange Houses

If it took 1,600 blocks to build each one of the 310 houses in a certain village, and 4,791 blocks to build a palace for the mayor, what kind of houses do the people live in? _____

11. What's a Round Ball?

A baseball is round, right? Well, in solving this problem you will be looking for a word beginning with "G" which describes the roundness of a ball.

Suppose a major league baseball team averages 43,800 fans per game for its 80 home games during the season, and another 4,079 fans showed up for an exhibition game. If you'll count up all the fans that watched that baseball team, you'll find that word. _____

12. Locking Them Up

In ancient days slaves were often transported by ship. In order to keep them secure the feet of the slaves were locked into a long bar with shackles. To discover the name of those ancient gadgets that held their feet, solve the following mathematical quiz on your calculator and read the result.

Twelve ships set sail from Africa with an average load of 295 slaves on each ship. The average weight of each slave was 143 pounds. If you will compute the total weight of all the slaves and add 2,498 to that figure, you will find the name of the ancient gadget that held their feet.

---

13. Did Santa Say That?

Bo: If Santa Claus stopped at 25,224,567 homes on his way across America on Christmas Eve, and each home had an average of 2 children who believed in him, what greetings did he leave for them?

Jo: I don't know. What?

Bo: Work it out on your calculator and you'll see they were hearty _____!

14. The Cow Jumped Over the Barn

Sam was visiting his uncle's farm and having a great time. He noticed a cow in the pasture. He asked the cow for her name but all she could say was "moo". That night in Sam's dream, the cow kept jumping over the barn. Sam counted the jumps in his sleep and was amazed to see her jump over the barn 400 times.

The next morning Sam carefully calculated the distance the cow would have to jump in order to accomplish the feat he had dreamed about. He found the distance to be 788.845 feet for each jump. Sam decided to add up the total number of feet this marvelous cow had jumped in his dream in order to find a name for her. _____

15. This Beats Counting Sheep!

Mildred was afflicted with insomnia. She tried counting birds so she could fall asleep. But all she could see was their feet, and she counted 70,678 of these. When she figured the number of birds, she discovered she had been counting

_____

16. What a Mess!

A huge tractor trailer carrying 1,000 cartons of eggs (each carton containing 2½ dozen eggs) collided with another tractor trailer carrying 11,752 gallons of molasses. Another tractor trailer, loaded with 8,037,166 chicken feathers, smashed into them. How would you describe the mess on the highway?

_____

17. What a Bird!

A certain bird watcher spotted an unusual bird. So he stopped to ask a native what it was.

"Well," replied the native, "if you will figure out how many seconds of time there are in 2 complete years of 365 days, and add to that figure 14,111,045 you will know the name of this strange bird and then you can look him up in the encyclopedia!" _____

18. He's Pretty Good at Golf

Tom was playing golf on an 18 hole course with an average distance of 531.8 yards per hole. His score was very good. He kept shooting par or below on every hole and he determined that he would keep playing until he played one hole that was above par. That didn't happen until he had played 3 complete rounds and 6 holes on the fourth round. What was Tom's score that final hole? _____

6

Having Fun
With Numbers

1. Let's Get to the Bottom of This!

A certain merchant in town put his product on 250 pairs of shoes and charged each customer $2.15. When he checked up, however, he found that one customer had paid only $1.70. When you figure out how much money he had, you'll also know what he was selling.

2. That's a Lot of Writing!

Jim started copying the Bible word for word when he was ten years old. He found that he could write an average of 110 words a minute. He worked 3 hours a day at his task over a period of 191 days. On the last day he finished a book by writing an additional 137 words. When you figure up the number of words Jim actually wrote you'll be amazed that his writing was still _____.

3. This Fellow Should Diet

Mr. Jones was a heavy eater. He started keeping a tally of the calories he consumed. For seven days he kept an accurate record and discovered that he averaged eating 5,674 calories every day. If you tally up his total calories for a week you'll discover a word that describes the protuberance around his stomach.

4. What a Vision!

John, the apostle of Jesus, was imprisoned in his old age. During this time he was privileged to see many visions of things that were to come, including a look into heaven itself. These visions are recorded in Revelation, the last book in the Bible.

In one of these visions he measured the new city of Jerusalem. He found that the city was square with 1500 miles on each side. The city had twelve gates so John just figured the circumference of the city and then the distance between each gate.

Assuming that an angel could walk faster than a human, suppose he set out to visit all the gates. On the first day he was able to walk far enough to visit seven gates, after leaving the first one. What's more, he traveled an additional 251 miles on his way to see the eighth gate. If you can figure out how many miles he traveled, you will know that John was imprisoned on the _____ of Patmos! If you miss, look it up in Rev. 1:9.

5. The Tribute Money

Matthew tells the story of the tax collector who came to Peter and asked "Doth not your master pay tribute?" (Matt. 17:24). Peter answered, "Yes", but he was not sure where Jesus would get the money to pay the taxes.

Jesus instructed Peter to go down to the sea and fish for the money. On the way, Peter was calculating in his mind how many fish he would have to catch to pay the tax bill.

"Suppose," he thought to himself, "I can sell each fish for $1.67. I will need to catch 46 fish and pay an extra $.37 out of my pocket in order to pay our taxes."

If you calculate what Peter would pay for the tax bill, you see he had misunderstood his Master's instructions. He thought he would find the money in the _____ of a fish. But all he had to do was catch one fish. Peter found the money for the tax bill in the fish's mouth (see Matt. 17:27).

6. Croaking Frogs

Tony was trying to sleep one night, but the croaking frogs kept him awake. He lay awake counting the croaks he heard. He estimated that the frogs were croaking an average of 300 times a minute. He listened for three (3) minutes and then counted 19 extra croaks. At this point, he jumped out of bed, dressed hurriedly, and started out of the house.

"Where are you going at this hour of the night?" he heard his father yelling.

"I'm going down to the pond to _____ some frogs!" he replied as he made his way outdoors.

7. What's In A Name?

Leroy met a girl at church. Naturally he asked, "What's your name?" She replied, "You figure it out." With that she handed him an essay to read with the following instructions: Find the letter of the alphabet that appears 1,276 times. Find another letter that appears 2,130 times. Find still another letter that appears 1,066 times and double it. Add all those figures together and you'll know my name is _____".

8. A Word for Jesus

John began his gospel by writing about the Word. He said, "In the beginning was the Word . . . and the Word was God" (John 1:1). John used a Greek word which is translated "the Word" in our Bible. Your job is to use your calculator to find that Greek word. Here's how to do it.

John said the Word (Jesus) was "in the beginning with God." Now, that was a long time ago, because God has always existed. But suppose we consider the creation of things as "the beginning" for our purposes and calculate the numbers in light years. Now a light year is the distance that light will travel in one year, an astronomical figure much too big to put into your calculator.

So we will use whole numbers to represent light years.

Suppose the world and the universe were created 20,000 light years ago. Now, suppose God created a place for the angels (Heaven) 30,907 light years before that. If you'll figure up all those light years you'll learn the Greek word John used in his gospel for Jesus.

9. Changing His Name

A certain young lad named
   Robert,
Thought he would change his
   name.
So, he took out his calculator,
And decided to play a game.

First, he entered seven-two,
   seven-two (7272).
That wasn't much of a job.
But when he divided that by
   nine,
He discovered his name was
   _____!

10. Ship Ahoy!

Paul, the apostle, was a man who got around. He traveled a lot. Sometimes he walked, sometimes he rode animals, and sometimes he sailed on ships.

On one occasion he was being taken to Rome as a prisoner on a ship, when a terrible storm came up. The ship's crew did everything they could to keep the ship afloat. They even _____ the mainsail. If you would like to discover an ancient term which means "to raise the sail" then work the problem and you'll find the answer.

There were 276 men aboard the ship (see Acts 27:37). They were ordered to throw all the cargo overboard to lighten the ship. Suppose each man threw

125 pounds of cargo overboard, and the anchors, which weighed 604 pounds together, were also thrown overboard. That should have lightened the ship enough for them to raise the sails. If you calculate all the weight that was thrown overboard you'll find that ancient word blinking in your calculator. Look it up in Acts 27:40 and read the rest of the story.

11. Milking Buffalo

Did you know they milk buffalo in India? It's a fact! And they make buffalo butter too! Your job is to find out what they call that buffalo butter in India.

Suppose it takes the milk from five (5) buffalo each day to make two (2) pounds of buffalo butter. How many buffalo would you need to produce 13,396 pounds of buffalo butter in ten days?

12. I've Got It!

Johnny was looking through a microscope at a drop of water. He was puzzled by the large number of organisms he saw swimming around in the water.

"What are those little wiggly things in the water?" he asked his science teacher.

"Those are amoeba," answered the teacher. "They are tiny one cell animals that multiply very rapidly by dividing. Imagine that three amoeba can each produce 372,371 other amoeba in one hour. Why, in just three hours those three amoeba alone will produce enough offspring to boggle the imagination!"

When Johnny figured up how many amoeba those three could produce in just three hours he exclaimed," _____ _____ _____ !"

13. That's Incredible!

You know, of course, that the whale is the largest mammal on earth. But consider the size of this huge creature by computing the value of its meat and oil.

Suppose a recent whaling expedition was able to harvest 14 of these huge creatures and that they averaged the following prices for the products gained from each whale. Each whale produced 200 gallons of whale oil which sells for $3.59 per gallon. The meat from each whale averaged 2,375 pounds at $1.89 per pound. In addition, each whale produced by-products valued at $1,354.06.

If you will calculate the total money involved in the sale of all fourteen whales you will discover that _____ _____
_____!

14. Some Gall!

David was bragging to a group of his friends about all the girls he had kissed. In the first grade he claimed he had kissed 53 girls; in the second grade, 175; in the third grade, 203; in the fourth grade, 337; in the fifth grade, 421; in the sixth grade, 937; in the seventh grade, 1,250; and in the eighth grade, 1,717.

Of course, David was stretching the truth a bit. But if you add up all his imaginary kisses you'll discover that a little bragging can sometimes help our male _____.

15. Whodunit?

The detective peered over his glasses at the young couple he was interrogating.

"Now, let's get this straight," he said. "You say that your boyfriend here has been robbing banks, but you didn't have anything to do with it, right?"

"Yes," the young girl sobbed. "He robbed the First National Bank and got $27,169.00; then he robbed the Federal Loan and Savings and got $15,960.00. Just a month ago he robbed the Citizens Bank and got $10,044.45!"

"She's wrong," interrupted the young man. "She robbed all those banks herself and tried to blame it on me. I didn't have anything to do with it!"

"No!" cried the young girl. "He's lying. I'm innocent of these charges!"

Meanwhile the detective was adding up all those figures on his calculator. When he finished, he arrested the young girl and booked her on the charge of bank robbery. Do you know why?

16. Who's the Best?

Sheila and Don were hoeing cotton in a gigantic cotton field. To find the answer to this problem you must solve two problems. First, find out how many chops Sheila made and write the answer down in two words. Then calculate the number of chops made by Don to complete the puzzle.

Sheila worked two weeks in the field. She worked 48 hours the first week and 50 hours the second week. She averaged 90 chops per minute. At the end of the second week Sheila worked a little extra by chopping an extra 1,234 times. Figure the total of Sheila's chops and write your answer in words in the first two blanks.

Don averaged only 60 chops per minute. He started out with good intentions but worked only 1 hour and 32 minutes. At the end of that time he chopped an extra 17 times and quit. When you calculate his total chops you'll discover that

_____ _____ _____.

17. You Need These For Walking

Tommy was studying anatomy. He read that a particular part of his body had so many blood vessels that if they were stretched out in one continuous line, they would travel a distance of 71,244 inches. If you'll reduce that figure to feet on your calculator you'll discover which part of his anatomy Tommy was studying.

18. Collector's Item

Mr. Higgins is a collector. Last year he spent $3,719.75 in his quest for the things he collects. He also spent $119.00 for advertising, and $27.00 for postage. But he sold $9,639.20 worth of his collection to other collectors. If you can figure out Mr. Higgin's profit for the year you will also know that he collects sea _____!

19. Trick or Treat!

Here's a numbers' trick you can use to baffle your friends on Halloween, or any other day of the year. With this trick you can amaze your friends by predicting the answer to a five column addition problem, and you will be right every time.

Ask your friend to think of any 4 or 5 digit number and write it down. Suppose he writes down the numbers 5734. To predict the answer in advance all you do is subtract 2 from that number and add a 2 to the front of the number. In this case your predicted answer would be 25,732. Write your predicted answer down, but do not reveal it to others yet.

Now, let your friend add another four digit number below that one. Suppose he adds 6,470. Tell your friend that you will add the next row of numbers. When you do, be sure that each number you add will total up to nine (9) when added to the number directly above it.

Now, ask your friend to add another row of numbers. You add the last row, being sure again that each number adds up to nine (9) with the number directly above it.

When you have finished putting down all the numbers, ask your friend to add up the columns on his calculator and he will be amazed to see that you predicted the right answer. Let's look at some examples.

5734   (Your predicted
        answer is 25,732)
6471   (Entered by your
        friend)

3528 (All numbers add up to nine with the row above it)

7105 (Entered by your friend)

2894 (All numbers add up to nine with the row above it)

25731 (Your predicted answer was right!)

Here's another example showing that the trick will work with any amount of numbers as long as you follow the rules for working the trick:

725,069 (Predicted answer is 2,725,067)

650,431

349,568

755,412

244,587

2,725,067

CAUTION: It is best to write the numbers down first and then use the calculator to add them up. You can use the calculator to work the trick, but it may be difficult to remember the numbers you needed to make the numbers add up to nine.

20. Surprise! Surprise!

Here's a trick with a surprise ending. You can do it with a friend. Ask your friend to enter any number, say a five digit number, in the calculator. Let your friend do all the steps in this trick, except the last one. Suppose your friend enters the number 25,732. Ask him to multiply by 2, add 4, multiply by 5, add 12, multiply by 10, and subtract 320.

At this point, take the calculator from your friend and remove all the final zeros by dividing by 10 repeatedly until they are gone. When you have removed all the final zeros, show the result to your friend. It will amaze him because it will be the exact number he started with!

Examples:

$$25,732 \times 2 + 4 \times 5 + 12 \times 10 - 320 = 25,732$$

$$14,561 \times 2 + 4 \times 5 + 12 \times 10 - 320 = 14,561$$

21. Twenty-three Shasham!

Here's a trick that will always end up with the same number—23.

Ask your friend to select any number (say a 4 or 5 digit number like 5,734 or 25,732) and put it in the calculator. Then ask him to add 25, multiply by 2, subtract 4, divide by 2, and subtract the original number.

The answer will always be 23 no matter what number you start with!

Examples:

25,732 + 25 × 2   4 : 2
    − 25,732 = 23
6,918 + 25 × 2 − 4 ÷ 2
    − 6,918 = 23

22. For Those Over Sixty

Here's another trick that will always end up with the same answer, in this case, 60.

Ask your friend to put any 2 digit number into the calculator. Instruct your friend to add 10, multiply by 2, add 100, divide by 2, and subtract the original number he started with. The answer will always be the same.

Examples:

11 + 10 × 2 + 100 ÷ 2 − 11 = 60

35 + 10 × 2 + 100 ÷ 2 − 35 = 60

77 + 10 × 2 + 100 ÷ 2 − 77 = 60

23. How Old Am I?

Once you have mastered this calculator trick you can tell anyone the month they were born in and how old they are! Sounds like fun you can have with many friends. Here's how you do it.

Ask your friend to enter the month of his birth in the calculator. If it was January it would be number 1, February, number 2, and so on, through the months of the year. Now, tell your friend that if he will faithfully execute your orders, you will not only tell him what month he was born in, but exactly how old he is too.

Ask your friend to multiply the number he has in the calculator by 10, add 20, multiply by 10, add 165, add his age, and subtract the number of days in a year, 365.

Now, look at the answer in the calculator. The last two digits will be your friend's age, and the first digit, or digits, will be the month of his birth. If your friend is less than 10 years old, then only the last single digit will be his age.

Examples:

For a man 49 years old who was born in December.

12 × 10 + 20 × 10 + 165 + 49 − 365 = 1249

For a child 8 years old, born in March.

3 × 10 + 20 × 10 + 165 + 49 − 365 = 308

For a youth 17 years old, born in June.

6 × 10 + 20 × 10 + 165 + 49 − 365 = 617

24. Starting All Over

Here's a numbers trick you can do yourself, or with friends.

Select any number and put it into the calculator, multiply by 2, add 4, multiply by 5, add 12, multiply by 10, subtract 320, and divide by 100.

Surprised? You'll always end up with the same number you started with!

Examples:

$55 \times 2 + 4 \times 5 + 12 \times 10 - 320 \div 100 = 55$

$32 \times 2 + 4 \times 5 + 12 \times 10 - 320 \div 100 = 32$

25. Starting All Over Again

Here's another way you can always end up with your original number.

Select any number and put it into the calculator. Multiply by 3, add 30, multiply by 5, add 600, divide by 15, and subtract 50.

Examples:

$347 \times 3 + 30 \times 5 + 600 \div 15 - 50 = 347$

$6,045 \times 3 + 30 \times 5 + 600 \div 15 - 50 = 6,045$

Answers*

Chapter One

1. Walking in the Woods
   $27 + 76 + 54 + 16 = 173$ (ELI)

2. An Ancestor for Joseph
   $6 \times 270 + 133 = 1,753$ (ESLI)

3. Caleb's Descendant
   $5,804 \times 5 + 20 = 1,451$ (ISHI)

4. Hosea's Other Name
   $785 + 60 \times 4 - 30 = 3,350$ (OSEE)

5. The Food Was Good!
   $201 \times 90 - 45 = 18,045$ (SHOBI)

6. David's Mighty Men
   $502,626 \div 6 - 37 = 83,734$ (HELEB)

7. The Man Who Lived a Long Time Ago
   $1,130 + 1,981 \times 365 - 397,801 =$
   $737,714$ (HILLEL)

8. A Fighting Man
   $27,900 + 30,600 + 14,673 = 73,173$
   (ELIEL)

9. The Son of Zerubbabel
   $190,840 \div 26 = 7,340$ (OHEL)

10. David's Camel Driver
    28,720 ÷ 4 = 7,180 (OBIL)

11. The King of Bashan's Bed
    7.5 × 6 × 2 = 90 (OG)

12. The Anti-Christ?
    666 + 144 (12 × 12) + 99 = 909 (GOG)

13. Joseph's Father
    $60 + $165 + $72 + $816 + $621 =
    $1,734 (HELI)

14. Jehoshaphat's Grandfather
    1,540 × 5 × 19 + 845
    = 147,145 (SHIL-HI)

15. This Name Will Amaze You
    1,000 × 2 × 2 × 2 × 2 × 2 × 2 × 2 × 2 ×
    2 × 2 × 2 × 2 + 441,345 = 4,537,345
    (SHELESH)

16. Sons of Benjamin
    22 (11 × 2) + 14 (7 × 2) + 24 + 17 + 20
    + 19 + 1 + 26 = 143 (EHI)

17. The Builder of Jericho
    18 × 67 + 13 × 6 = 7,314 (HIEL)

18. How Lucky Can You Get?
    150 + 160 + 170 + 180 + 190 + 200 +
    210 + 220 + 230 + 240 + 250 + 260 +
    270 + 280 + 290 + 300 + 334 = 3,934
    (HEGE)

19. Timothy's Godly Grandmother
    12 x 365.25 x 70 ÷ 60 − 6 = 5,107
    (LOIS)

Chapter Two

1. What An Awful Place!
   7,733 + 1 = 7,734 (HELL)

2. This Fellow Was Smart
   138 + 210 + 307 + 79 + 204 = 938
   (BEG)

3. Golgotha
   5,354 + 964 + 1,396 = 7,714 (HILL)

4. The Tabernacle in the Wilderness
   376,300 + 30,845 = 407,145 (SHILOH)
   see Joshua 18:1

5. The Prodigal Son
   $1,260 + $2,960 + $1,500 + $184 =
   $5,904 (HOGS)

6. John the Baptist
   $3{,}045 + 50{,}000 = 53{,}045$ (SHOES)

7. The Serpent in the Garden
   $1{,}675 + 2{,}050 + 1{,}275 + 515 - 1 = 5{,}514$ (HISS)

8. Samson's Riddle
   $\$46.98 + \$6.40 = \$53.38$ (BEES)

9. Everyone Should Read This Book
   $66 \times 5.73 = 378.18$ (BIBLE)

10. The Devil and His Angels
    $12 \times 5{,}862 + 1 = 70{,}345$ (SHEOL)

11. The False God
    $41 \times 18 = 738$ (BEL)

12. What a Place for a Battle!
    $3{,}232 \div 4 + 1 = 809$ (GOB)

13. Moses' Ultimatum
    $148.875 \times 24 = 3{,}573$ (ELSE)

14. Ahithophel's Hometown
    $13{,}500 \times 3 + 219 = 40{,}719$ (GILOH)

15. More Than Knowledge
    31,101 × 172 + 6,006 = 5,355,378
    (BLESSES)

16. The Walls of Jericho Came Tumbling
    Down
    A. 151,213 × 13 × 2 = 3,931,538
       (BESIEGE)
    B. 151,213 × 26 = 3,931,538
       (BESIEGE)

17. The Cry From the Cross
    521 − 9 × 2 + 19 − 1,073 (ELOI)

18. Goliath
    126(10.5 × 12) + 622 + 150 + 20 = 918
    (BIG)

19. Job's Afflictions
    14,553 + 10,790 + 31,765 = 57,108
    (BOILS)

20. Which Way Is Up?
    5,280 × 12 ÷ 3 − 16,206 = 4,914
    (HIGH)

21. This One Is Taxing
12,575,200 + 15,490,515
+ 31,026,743 × $.64
= 37,819,173 (ELIGIBLE)

22. Stretching the Truth
91 × 345 + 343 = 31,738 or 92 × 345 −
2 = 31,738 (BELIE)

23. Consider the Flowers in the Field
314 (366 − 52) × $16.48 + 142.45 =
$5,317.17 (LILIES)

Chapter Three

1. A Sad Story
5 × 161 = 805 (SOB)

2. Land Hungry
2,000 + 340 + 2,175 + 794 = 5,309
(GOES)

3. A Disaster!
$10.31 + $25.80 + $26.07 + $15.00 =
$77.18 (BILL)

4. Church Musician
70 × 44 = 3,080 (OBOE)

5. Special Entertainment
   $101.41 \times 5 = \$507.05$ (SOLOS)

6. That's A Lotta' Books
   $39{,}851 \times 8 = 318{,}808$ (BOBBIE)

7. This Preacher Got Around!
   $25 \times 19{,}655 = 491{,}375$ (SLEIGH)

8. Who's Keeping the Books?
   $\$6{,}077 \times 52 + \$1{,}714 = \$317{,}718$
   (BILLIE)

9. The Handshaker
   $4{,}882 \times 2 \times 52 + 6 = 507{,}734$
   (HELLOS)

10. The Church Parsonage
    $\$4{,}100 \times 3 + \$26{,}079 = \$38{,}379$
    (GLEBE)

11. What A Church Can Do
    $13{,}832 \div 52 \div 7 = 38$ (BE)

12. What Are Those Strange Sounds?
    $520 (10 \times 52) \times 111 + 18 = 57{,}738$
    (BELLS)

13. The Lost Sermon
   $25 \times 300 + 215 = 7,715$ (SILL)

14. The Right Word
   $304,290 \div 6 = 50,715$ (SILOS)

15. Mysterious Occupation
   A. $80 + 50 + 215 = 345$ (SHE)
   B. $346.25 + $162.10 + $25.72 +
      $43.28 = $577.35 (SELLS)
   C. $2,652.25 \times 20\% = $530.45 or
      $2,652.25 \div 5 = $530.45 (SHOES)

16. Plastered With Money!
   $2,750 \times $1.75 + $242.89 = $5,055.39
   (GESSOS)

17. What's He Doing?
   $61 + 189 + 51 \times 22 \times 7 + 3,691 =
   50,045$ (SHOOS)

18. That Should Make It Shine!
   $60 \times $7.95 + $63.00 (21 \times $3.00) +
   $10.79 = $550.79 (GLOSS)

19. Happily Married
   $708.5 (13 \times 54.5) + 1117.4 (37 \times 30.2)
   + 706.8 (62 \times 11.4) + 2817.5 (49 \times
   57.5) + 84.8 + 82.8 = 5517.8$ (BLISS)

Chapter Four

1. Cover Him Up!
   $3.98 + $2.79 + $1.41 = $8.18 (BIB)

2. He Couldn't Work That Day
   10 + 20 + 21 + 721 − 1 = 771 (ILL)

3. She's a Mean Woman
   335 + 475 + 7 = 817 (LIB)

4. Achilles Had a Tender Spot
   3,762 + 2,531 + 1,041 = 7,334 (HEEL)

5. He Traveled a Lot
   $21,560 + $11,404 + $604 + $4,511 = $38,079 (GLOBE)

6. How's That Again?
   24 + 15 + 4 = 43 (EH)

7. What a Job!
   $54,108 ÷ 12 = $4,509 (GOSH)

8. Too Many Chiefs
   493 + 100 + 11,576 + 57,102 + 276,593 + 176,936 + 12,708 = 535,508 (BOSSES)

9. Facts Don't Mean a Thing
   $3,750 - 2,842 = 908$ (BOG)

10. Traveling Men
    $27,000 + 15,000 + 5,304 + 3,500 = 50,804$ (HOBOS)

11. Silly Girl
    $\$1,574.50 + \$269.00 + \$1,500.00 + \$455.69 = \$3,799.19$ (GIGGLE)

12. A Staggering Thought
    $\$79,780.68 \div 21 = \$3,799.08$ (BOGGLE)

13. New Boy In Town
    $507,734 - 15,488 \div 69 = 7,134$ (HEIL)

14. A Beautiful Girl
    $100 \times 365 + 1,238 = 37,738$ (BELLE)

15. Make a Joyful Noise
    $61 \times 55 + 24 = 3,379$ (GLEE)

16. This Man Is Hungry
    $12,300 \times 364 + 42,704 = 4,519,904$ (HOGGISH)

17. These Ladies Have a Problem
$$2,025 (15 \times 135) + 1,692 (12 \times 141) +$$
$$5,250 (35 \times 150) + 4,960 (32 \times 155) +$$
$$6,880 (43 \times 160) + 5,115 (31 \times 165) +$$
$$4,590 (27 \times 170) + 2,625 (15 \times 175) +$$
$$1,080 (6 \times 180) + 555 (3 \times 185) + 380$$
$$(2 \times 190) + 228 = 35,380 \text{ (OBESE)}$$

18. Televisionitus!
$$360 \times 15 + 2,608 (652 \times 4) = 8,008$$
(BOOB)

19. What a Job He Has!
   A. $1977 - 1943 = 34$ (HE)
   B. $3,264 (8 \times 12 \times 34) \times 17.5 + 615$
      $= 57,735$ (SELLS)
   C. $\$203,762 \div 34 = 5,993$ (EGGS)

Chapter Five

1. He Didn't Catch Much
   $\$4.52 + \$1.79 + \$1.02 = \$7.33$ (EEL)

2. Call Him Something
   $126,600 + 126,700 + 126,609 =$
   $379,909$ (GOGGLE)

3. He Was a Smooth Talker
   $376 + 1,562 + 79 + 1,750 + 2,089 + 1,915 + 408 = 8,179$ (GLIB)

4. How's This For Dessert?
   $369.5 \times 2 = 739$ (GEL)

5. The Mysterious Holes
   $10 \times 71 = 710$ (OIL)

6. Wild Crowd
   $36,962 - 31,954 = 5,008$ (BOOS)

7. What a Gander!
   $1,000 \times 35 + 9 = 35,009$ (GOOSE)

8. The Fields Are White
   $274 \times 49 \times 4 + 4 = 53,708$ (BOLES)

9. Cry Baby
   $1,059 + 3,759 \times 658 + 1,833,764 = 5,004,008$ (BOO HOOS)

10. Strange Houses
    $1,600 \times 310 + 4,791 = 500,791$ (IGLOOS)

11. What's a Round Ball?
    43,800 × 80 + 4,079 = 3,508,079
    (GLOBOSE)

12. Locking Them Up
    12 × 295 × 143 + 2,498 = 508,718
    (BILBOS)

13. Did Santa Say That?
    25,224,567 × 2 = 50,449,134
    (HEIGH HOS)

14. The Cow Jumped Over the Barn
    400 × 788.845 = 315,538 (BESSIE)

15. This Beats Counting Sheep!
    70,678 ÷ 2 = 35,339 (GEESE)

16. What A Mess!
    30,000 (1,000 × 30) + 11,752 +
    8,037,166 = 8,078,918 (BIG BLOB)

17. What A Bird!
    365 × 2 × 24 × 60 × 60 + 14,111,045 =
    77,183,045 (SHOEBILL)

18. He's Pretty Good at Golf
    60 (3 × 18 + 6) × 531.8 = 31,908
    (BOGIE)

Chapter Six

1. Let's Get to the Bottom of This
   $$249 \,(250 - 1) \times \$2.15 + \$1.70 = \$537.05 \text{ (SOLES)}$$

2. That's a Lot of Writing
   $$110 \times 60 \times 573 \,(3 \times 191) + 137 = 3{,}781{,}937 \text{ (LEGI-BLE)}$$

3. This Fellow Should Diet
   $$5{,}674 \times 7 = 39{,}718 \text{ (BILGE)}$$

4. What a Vision!
   $$1500 \times 4 \div 12 \times 7 + 251 = 3{,}751 \text{ (ISLE)}$$

5. The Tribute Money
   $$\$1.67 \times 46 + \$.37 = \$77.19 \text{ (GILL)}$$

6. Croaking Frogs
   $$3 \times 300 + 19 = 919 \text{ (GIG)}$$

7. What's In a Name?
   1,276 + 2,130 + 2,132
   (1,066 × 2) = 5,538 (BESS)

8. A Word For Jesus
   20,000 + 30,907 = 50,907
   (LOGOS)

9. Changing His Name
   7,272 ÷ 9 = 808 (BOB)

10. Ship Ahoy!
    276 × 125 + 604 =
    35,104 (HOISE)

11. Milking Buffalo?
    13,396 ÷ 10 × 2.5 =
    3,349.00 (GHEE)

12. I've Got It!
    3 × 372,371 × 3 =
    3,351,339 (GEE I SEE)

13. That's Incredible!
    $718.00 (200 × $3.59) +
    $4,488.75 (2,375 × $1.89)
    + $1,354.06 × 14 =
    $91,851.34 (HE IS BIG)

14. Some Gall!
    53 + 175 + 203 + 337 +
    421 + 937 + 1,250 +
    1,717 = 5,093 (EGOS)

15. Whodunit?
    $27,169.00 + 15,960.00
    + $10,044.45 =   =
    $53,173.45 (SHE LIES)

16. Who's the Best?
    48 + 50 × 60 × 90 +
    1,234 = 530,434 (HE
    HOES)
    60 + 32 × 60 + 17 =
    5,537 (LESS)

17. You Need These For Walk-
    ing
    71,244 ÷ 12 = 5,937
    (LEGS)

18. Collector's Item
    $9,639.20 − $3,719.75 −
    $119.00 − $27.00 =
    $5,773.45 (SHELLS)

Recommended further reading:

If you enjoyed this book, we suggest that you order one or more of the following titles. You can order these books by sending a check directly to: **Mott Media, 1000 East Huron, Milford, MI 48042,** (Include 6% for postage and handling.)

Four Trojan Horses of Humanism, by Harry Conn. The author shares his thoughts and opinions with those who dare to think. True Christianity is worth dying for, but this will not be perceived until it (Christianity) has been purged of cheap grace, easy believism, and humanistic motives brought in by the theological Trojan Horse.

The Separation Illusion, by John Whitehead. Refutes the commonly-held belief that religion must be separated from government and applies this discussion to the court decisions on prayer and Bible reading in public schools.

Are Textbooks Harming Your Children? by James Hefley. Shocking quotes of the materials discovered by the Gablers in their reviews of public school texts. Informative information is given on how you, parents like themselves, can take action to improve American Education.

How to Tutor, by Samuel L. Blumenfeld. The book is divided into four parts: how to qualify as a tutor, reading primer, writing primer, and arithmetic primer. Useful for tutoring children at the preschool level as a preventive measure during the first two grades of public school as a supplement to the child's instruction, or for use in remedial instruction at any grade level. Paper,

A Christian Approach to Education, by H.W. Bryne. An outstanding survey of the basic theories of Christian education. This is a new approach based on Biblical principles and compares the secular and Christian views of education prevalent today.

Asking Questions: A Classroom Model for Teaching the Bible, by D. Bruce Lockerbie. Each question leads to a variety of responses intended to teach, first, what the text says; then, what it means; and finally how its principles apply to Bible readers today.

Handbook on Athletic Perfection, by Wes Neal. "The perfect athletic performance can only be experienced by the Christian athlete controlled by the Holy Spirit who has been sent by God to develop Jesus Christ's attitudes and actions in your athletic performance as well as your entire life." Biblical premise for every principle stated and practical applications of those principles.

Handbook on Coaching Perfection, by Wes Neal. Thesis is "use me Lord to draw recognition back to you." Emphasis is on seeking what Scripture says and then doing things (even coaching) God's way. Excellent gift for coaches, athletes.

Teach Them Diligently, A Devotional Guide for Teachers Who Care, by Arthur Nazigian. Presents concisely many ways to identify the blessings of God in your educational ministry. You will be blessed each time you meditate through the book.

The Sower Series of World Heroes
Character-building Christian Biographies for Young Readers:

George Washington Carver—Man's Slave Becomes God's Scientist, by David R. Collins. Read the astounding story of one man's rise from slavery and the struggles and triumphs of his faith.

Francis Scott Key—God's Courageous Composer, by David R. Collins. Loyal American patriot, defender of God's Word, writer of our National Anthem. Francis Scott Key's life was full of challenges . . . learn of how God cares for His own.

Christopher Columbus, by Bennie Rhodes. An exciting book about a Christian explorer who sought to discover new lands to spread the gospel at the risk of shipwreck, disease, and personal failure.

Robert E. Lee, by Lee Roddy. A Christian of impeccable character, Lee became one of the most respected men in America—even in the face of defeat.

Abigail Adams, by Evelyn Witter. The story of the wife of America's second President whose personal faith in Christ kept her strong in a young war torn nation.

George Washington, by Norma Cournow Camp. The story of the first President who was not a great preacher or Bible scholar, but who patterned his own life around the Bible lessons he studied daily. He was a sower of seeds of faith and courage.

Johannes Kepler, by John Hudson Tiner. This giant of faith and science considered his scientific studies to be another way of looking into God's creation.

Isaac Newton, by John Hudson Tiner. Here is the life story of the astronomer and mathematician who discovered the law of gravity and who was a devout, Bible-believing Christian.

Abraham Lincoln, David R. Collins. A true sower of faith and freedom, this biography describes Abe's experiences in his search for an understanding of God.

Available from your local Christian bookstore or from **Mott Media, 1000 East Huron, Milford, MI 48042 (Phone Toll Free: 1–800–521–4350; or in MI 313–685–8773)**